The Dangers of Prayerlessness

A 30 DAY DEVOTIONAL TO REIGNITE YOUR PRAYER LIFE

Dorothy V. McIntosh

The Dangers of Prayerlessness

© 2017 Divine Works Publishing

All rights reserved. No part of this publication may be reproduced, stored in a retrieval system or transmitted in any form or by any means, electronic, mechanical, photocopying, recording or otherwise without the prior permission of the publisher or in accordance with the provisions of the Copyright, Designs and Patents Act 1988 or under the terms of any license permitting limited copying issued by the Copyright Licensing Agency.

ISBN-13: 978-0-9996047-2-4 (paperback)

Published by:
Divine Works Publishing
Royal Palm Beach, Florida USA
www.divineworkspublishing.com
561-990-BOOK (2665)

Dedication

I dedicate this book in loving memory of my dear mother, Evangelist Evelyn A. McIntosh, my first prayer teacher, a great intercessor and a courageous saint- who with great zeal, gave her service and devotion to our Lord Jesus. Thank you, mummy; for passing down the mantle. I know that you are looking down and cheering me on with the heavenly host of witnesses.

To my late, adopted and spiritual mother Evangelist Enamae Parker, a mighty prayer warrior and a great evangelist. Thank you for being a shining example of faith, hope, and love.

I dedicate this book in honor of my precious father, Rev. Ezekiel A. McIntosh Sr., whose great zeal of faith, contagious love, prayers, and support has steered and kept me focused in my pursuit of God. Thank you, daddy, I love you.

Last, but most important, this book is dedicated to my Lord and King, Jesus Christ. Thank you, Jesus; for apprehending and liberating me. My soul follows hard after you.

Endorsements

The author Dr. Dorothy McIntosh is a God seeker. This has been proven throughout the hard trials of her life. In this powerful devotional she admonishes and encourages us to give ourselves to prayer above all. In her deep pursuit of God, she understands that prayer is the basis for a lifestyle of godliness and it reveals His divine nature and high calling. It refreshes the life of the believer and keeps him in tune with Holy Spirit.

She is indeed a great testimony to the lack of prayer through her own personal experiences and is now living a purposeful life through the awesome power of prayer. It is my hope that purpose be fulfilled in your life, as you accept the challenge to make prayer a priority.

Chief Apostle Dr. H. L. Smith
Pentecostal Deliverance Fellowship Ministry Inc.

The Dangers of Prayerlessness is an easy to read two-fold devotional, designed to ignite a passion for personal prayer while creating an atmosphere of intimacy to develop the faith of the believer. I believe that this devotional will not only equip and challenge you in the arena of prayer but it will also enhance your walk with The Lord.

Apostle Valentine Johnson
Kingdom Life Ministries

This Book, "The Dangers of Prayerlessness", is an awakening to the need and importance of prayer as Christians. It gives directives on how to pray the various types of prayer for a setting or circumstances. One can really nourish their soul and spirit if they follow this awakening call to prayer.

This book places strong emphasis on prayer and detailed reasons why we must pray. While the many types of prayer are pointed out, each line in the text is very much self-explanatory, yet each line is a topic from which volumes can be written, making the contents lesson that can be taught.

The Christian who is struggling can find great sources of courage and strength, and corrections for one self. One of the key factors that this book contributes to is Spiritual Discipline. The lack of Spiritual Discipline is a serious weakness among Christians. The author of this book helps you with that.

The few pages are power packed with guidelines on how to use your spiritual war weaponry if you would only submit to the various form of prayer as needed. Having complied with the instructions given in this book, it would produce a well refined Christian, Mission oriented, Purpose Driven and Rapture ready.

I hereby endorse this Book for the purpose of Ministry

Kenneth Major Jr.
Dr. of Theology C.C.M.A

FOREWORD

Dorothy McIntosh is a woman of prayer and a heart for God. Her book is infused with her passion and her desire for Christians to return to prayer. The Dangers of Prayerlessness is inspiring, encouraging, and challenging to all believers. The author reminds us that prayer is not an option but the mainstay of the Christian life. This is great resource to help believers to have a more effective prayer life or to make prayer a priority.

Dr. Erick Brookins
Pastor, Surfside Community Fellowship

ACKNOWLEDGEMENTS

I want to thank my family, Kendra Marie, Krystal Lakeisha, Kristan, Christopher and Kristoin, for their patience and tremendous support with this project.

Special thanks to the dedicated mothers and sisters of St. Thomas Baptist Church: Naomi & Maureen McIntosh, Deborah McKenzie, the late Aremintha Curry, Monvella Pinder and Ismay Pedican who labored with me during 5 a.m. prayer.

Thank you also to Bishop Burnell Parker, my sister Roslyn Russell, special ministry friends, Evangelist Katrina Thompson and Prophet Delvano McIntosh for their unselfish support, tremendous sacrifices and continuous encouragement in my persistent chase after God. I love you all.

Over the years I have had the opportunity to sit at the feet of many great men and women who inspired me through their teachings on the importance of prayer in the life of the believer. Special thanks to my mentoring Pastor, Dr. Kenneth Major Jr., Bishop Cardinal McIntosh, Bishop Ricardo Grant, Apostles Edward & Lee Watson and Apostle Alex & Minister Brenda Archer.

My deepest gratitude goes to one of the greatest Global Kingdom Ambassadors. She's a mentoring mother in the gospel, who has over the years poured tremendous words of wisdom, counsel and spiritual insights into my life unselfishly. She is a mother of mothers; an advocate for change; a woman of unfeigned faith and prophetic movements; a giant and general in the kingdom of Jehovah. I salute Apostle Collamae Collymore (aka Mama Cola).

To a wonderful Professor who has been in my life since the age of five (5) years old; my Big Brother "Benji," whose profound knowledge and revelatory interpretation of the Word of God has impacted and empowered my life and has indeed played a significant role in this assignment. Heartfelt thanks for your patience, humility and brotherly love over the years. Many many Blessings!

Introduction

This particular message has been in my spirit for many years.

In 1999, while faced with multiple challenges, the Lord gave me a vision at five o'clock one morning. In the vision, I was upstairs in the house that once belonged to my deceased grandparents. The room was extremely dark; I opened the western wooden window to get a radiance of moonlight, but to my surprise, the moon was not glowing.

While questioning the Lord concerning the difficulties I was experiencing at that time, He spoke these words to me, "Your cord is broken." I did not comprehend the prophetic message. At this point, I looked out the window toward the south, and something grabbed my attention. It was a huge bright light shining around the margins of a square-shaped field where my grandfather once grew vegetables. There I saw the shadow of a man walking in the luminosity.

I looked closer and was amazed to have recognized that it was Bishop Cardinal McIntosh, marching vigorously and praying passionately. It was as if he were warfaring on my behalf. Immediately I understood the words Holy Spirit had just spoken to me.

"My prayer cord was disconnected." I had become overwhelmed with responsibilities and worries; I found little or (sometimes) no time to pray. My life was going downhill. Reality hit in; if I desired to be like Jesus, (which I did), then a prayer life was mandatory.

As a result of this vision, I have made a conscientious decision regarding my future walk with God. I began planning each day with prayer as my top priority. I committed to meet with God at five o'clock every morning and also throughout the day. I started experiencing newness in Him, and my prayer cord mended.

As you read this book, I pray that you are encouraged to spend quality time in prayer and become intimate with your Father. Believe me, your life will never be the same again.

Pass this book on to others.

TABLE OF CONTENTS

Introduction xiii
The Enemy's Virus xviii
Maintaining Balance in Your Quest for God xxiii
Prayer Has Atomic Power xxiv
Itinerating One's Prayer Life xxix
Become a God Seeker xxxi

DEVOTIONALS

Day 1 Broken Relationship *1*
Day 2 Connect with God *5*
Day 3 Knowing and Understanding His Word *9*
Day 4 Live in the Spirit *13*
Day 5 Faith Works through Love *17*
Day 6 Perseverance *21*
Day 7 The Revelation of His Word *25*
Day 8 Believing Fully in the Father *29*
Day 9 Love Toward the Father *33*
Day 10 The Way to God *37*
Day 11 Abiding in the Vine *41*
Day 12 The Peace of God *45*
Day 13 Commanded to Love *49*
Day 14 Trust His Grace *53*
Day 15 Rivers of Living Water *57*
Day 16 Your Authority in God *61*
Day 17 Alive unto God *65*
Day 18 He Restores My Soul *69*
Day 19 Watchman on the Wall *73*
Day 20 Being Reconciled to God *77*
Day 21 Courage in Suffering *81*
Day 22 Hearing and Obeying *85*
Day 23 Suffering to Become Like Him *89*
Day 24 Shake it Off *93*
Day 25 Deliverance *97*
Day 26 Praise that Moves God *101*
Day 27 What is Obstructing your Flow? *105*
Day 28 Consecrate Yourselves *109*
Day 29 Never Doubt God *113*
Day 30 The Wise in Character *117*

The Enemy's Virus

COMBAT THE INFECTION OF PRAYERLESSNESS WITH THE INJECTION OF PRAYER

(Virus: a tiny parasite, disease-causing or infective agent; sinful or destructive influence that contaminates or poisons the mind or character;)

For centuries in the physical realm, germ warfare has been conducted among warring countries. Similarly in the spirit realm the enemy of our souls has been raging a virus like campaign with a death like initiative. This destructive latent debilitating virus is nothing more than carelessness in the life of the believer. The virus of prayerlessness is most imperturbable and dangerously subtle in its approach. This disease targets every believer specifically those who are distracted with self-interest. It has no regard for your rank or station but seeks to contaminate the very core of your soul with a principal intent to pollute and terminate your spiritual walk with God.

According to the Apostle Peter, the only sure and certain remedy for this condition is vigilance, to discipline you in the engagement of prayerfulness, (1 Peter 5:8).

There are two cords that bind the people of God to Satan's cart; the things of duty and the pleasures of sin. It is a sad reality the average believer today has multiplicity of duties and responsibilities so overwhelming that without being conscious they forget to pray.

To put it succinctly the enemy's strategy is to complicate your lives with meaningless, trivial things that causes you to undervalue prayer time with God. It is of vital importance for you to understand that you are just being spiritually lazy and complacently indifferent; in other words you have lost your first love.

It is no mystery therefore that, gross deficiency in prayer results in latent spiritual bankruptcy which is a definite act of suicide to the very life of the believer. Such believers under the disguise of prayerlessness unconsciously surrender themselves to the fiery darts of the enemy. Little wonder then why the scripture said he is as a "roaring lion seeking whom he may devour."

It is expected therefore that a mature seasoned warfaring believer stay in a continuous ever advancing intimacy with God in prayer. It is our Father's ultimate will that every born again believer emulate our Savior in this prayer relationship. Here the old bromide is still true (more prayer, more power).

Thus, the equation is very simple; a prayerful life equals a powerful life in the Spiritual Arena. The Bible declares in Romans 8:37, "We are more than conquerors through Him (Christ) who loved us."

In other words, we have power over the enemy. This power comes only through a prayer full life.

Constantly praying the word of God goes to the core of the problem and destroys this bug. Saints of the kingdom, be encouraged and resort to our Father through a lifestyle of prayer.

Maintaining Balance in Your Quest for God

THE LORD TAKES PLEASURE IN AUTHENTIC WEIGHTS

Maintaining balance means to retain equilibrium, stability, and steadiness.

Prayer should never be replaced with any other spiritual discipline because they are intertwined and intricately connected. In the book of Acts the record shows a worthy example of Paul and Silas. After being tortured and in immense pain, at midnight their voices resounded in solemn prayer and high praise to our heavenly Father. The record is clear, regardless of your present situation, or varied circumstances, trial or tribulation the true child of God can still maintain his/her composure being assured they are still "dwelling in the secret place of the Most High."

It is ultimately your utmost responsibility to maintain a place of refuge that the enemy cannot infuriate nor penetrate.

Further on the matter of balance, Proverbs 11:1 says, "a false (or deceitful) balance is an abomination to the Lord: but a just weight is his delight," KJV. The Lord abhors dishonest scales, but an accurate weight is His delight," NETB. When the adversary of your soul "Satan" himself releases his assaults against you, you need power that can only be bestowed through falling on your knees.

Allow nothing to create an imbalance within your prayer life. Devote your itinerary to Holy Spirit.

Prayer Has Atomic Power

THE IMPELLING DUTY OF PRAYER PROVIDES INFINITE POWER

Prayer is an address, an earnest request; it is entreating the Lord; a call upon His name. Prayer is a quest, and it is expected of us. We have been indicted by a divine summons to erect an altar to resort to in prayer. Stressing the importance of continuous prayer our Savior gave direction to the eleven apostles to pursue the presence of God through prayer. Recognizing that failure to do so would render them weak and vacillating and unable to comprehend, much less to appreciate spiritual battles that they were to encounter.

The bible instructs us in Luke 18:1, "Men ought always to pray and not to faint," KJV. This calls for fervency and persistency. When your soul desire and passion is ultimately consumed with doing the will of God as Jesus said, "I delight to do Thy will oh my God: yea thy law is within my heart," a productive life is the ultimate result.

Prayer can be described as a war engine with atomic power to erupt an earth quake in your prison cell, causing a jail break and crushing every chain that have you bound. Prayer empowers you to access divine arsenals and hence intercept, dismantle, annihilate, and destroy demonic plots and plans set against your destiny.

Prayer is the instrument of spiritual power which positions you to receive spiritual insights and specific directions to your divine destination. It is also the power tool that arms you to assassinate demonic undertakings in the earth realm. Such was the experience as seen in the life of Elijah the Tishbite. Apart from commanding that no rain or no dew would fall for three years until he says so, he through the power of prayer summoned instantly the visible fiery demonstration of God through prayer-instantly. The arsenal of prayer with active use in the hand of the believer enables heaven to invade earth. "Let Your Kingdom come and Your will be done on earth as it is in heaven." Matthew 6:10. Your successful spiritual journey is inevitably in direct proportion to the vitality and urgency of your prayer life.

It causes great pain in the soul when you realize that the mission of prayer has been relegated not only to the last but to the least of Christian engagement and pursuit. To the believer prayer is not a suggestion or even a recommendation; it is a divine authoritative command from the Eternal Himself. It is an unspoken reality that too many believers regard prayer as a last resort. In other words, you wait until you are faced with an adverse circumstance to pray. It is mandated that you establish your altar of prayer unto God instantaneously.

Through the spiritual exercises of engaging in praise, offering of prayers and uncontaminated worship, you summon the divine presence of God to your environment. You must therefore, "gird up the loins of your minds," shake off the dust of lethargy and laodiceanism, arise from your position of complacency and cry out to Abba-Father. At those times when you feel less inclined to pray it is at such times you must need to pray.

To abandon prayer is to invite feebleness and is nothing short of endeavoring to wage spiritual warfare in your own strength and power. Again reference is made to our Savior's high value on prayer- Luke 5:16 tells us," But Jesus often withdrew to lonely places and prayed," much more you as sinful beings need to prayer. There is no way of escaping this inevitability. Whenever and wherever you as a believer lose your desire for close intimacy in prayer with God, you find yourself engaged in a round of useless activities and a host of non-essential, unprofitable distracting enterprises.

Prayer then should be unceasing, unhesitatingly, relentless and with great specificity. Prayer must also be so absorbing in your spiritual system so that your communion with God remains constant. Praying without ceasing then simply means that regardless of the vicissitudes and challenges of daily life, you ought to be in constant direct communication with your Heavenly Father.

Prayer is essentially a command from God; failure to pray then is nothing short of lack of faith and sin. For the scripture records that, "whatsoever is not of faith is sin," Romans 14:23b.

ITINERATING ONE'S PRAYER LIFE

PERSISTENTLY PLAN FOR PRODUCTIVE RESULTS

Plan according to Webster's dictionary is a method or scheme of acting, doing, or arranging. It also means to make a decision about one's futuristic intent.

As surely as you neglect to – make no provisions to meet God in prayer, you would just as surely fail to meet God and engage in prayer. You must schedule daily prayer time. Our attention is drawn to the age old adage, "one's failure to plan is a plan to fail." If you are going to efficiently and effectively accomplish your God-given purpose then planning is of great necessity. The consequence of not planning brings distress and consternation. In this environment there are created avenues that makes it easier for the enemy to infiltrate, confuse and infuriate the prayer less one. Your determination and strategies will bring productivity and success. Proverbs 21:5 reads, "The plans of the diligent lead surely to abundance" -ESV. Determination not desire controls your destiny. To be a competent prayer warrior, it is required to have communion with God daily.

Prayer is never a course of action, but a necessary spiritual discipline that you must embrace as a believer. Remember, to live a Godly life prayer is the order of the day. To do otherwise is to prove to be a dishonor to God and a reproach to one's spiritual walk.

Become A God Seeker

HE REWARDS THE DILIGENT

When your life becomes crowded with many demands, make sure the first thing you do every day is to seek God in prayer. Even though your life may be overwhelmed with cares, duties and responsibilities, you are to ensure that above all things you seek the Lord daily. As in all things spiritual, God does not only desire but requires diligence and consistency-consistency is a jewel. It is impossible to hold God responsible for deficiency on your part if you fail to spend quality and consistent time in this exercise of prayer. To rush off in a hurried touchdown way will not bring the spiritual results you are seeking. God will make your effort of prayer worthwhile when you invest time in His presence. In so doing you will experience the promise as recorded in Romans 12:2, "be not conformed to this world but be ye transformed by the renewing of your mind, that you may prove what is that good, and acceptable, and perfect will of God."

"He is a rewarder of all that diligently seek Him." Hebrews 11:6. As Kingdom Ambassadors, it is imperative that you avoid the business of seeking your own way and means when you ought to be seeking diligently the Master's will. Without question He must have preeminence in our life for there is none like Him and He is never satisfied with nothing less than our all and all. In other words any partial sacrifice or blemished offerings or halfhearted service in any department of your life is not recognized much less sanctioned by your Father in heaven. In answering our prayers at times even as He did in the days of Elijah He will manifest His glory and in so doing honor the one that is honoring Him. He did the same for Daniel in the lion's den, the three Hebrews worthies and Nehemiah in the court of Artaxerxes the king of Persia. Prayer is indeed the means of spending treasured time with God. When you do this, your life will become more valuable and successful. You will continuously experience increase, expand and accelerate. Prayer is the way you express your inner thoughts to your heavenly Father. Fervent prayer illuminates His plan and will for your life. Jeremiah 29:11 says, "For I know the plans I have for you, declares the Lord, plans for your welfare and not for your calamity, to give you a future and a hope." (NASB).

Prayer will ultimately revolutionize your entire perspective on life. And in this way the Father is able to render unto the diligent seeker the boundless treasures of heaven's storehouse. Ponder this, Prayer is essentially the nuts and bolts, and all of the spiritual mechanized agencies to reveal and empower one to execute the divine blueprint and thereby bring you into the will of the architect of the Universe. Time spent in prayer provides the preordained vital strategies making it necessary for you to meet and to disarm the enemy of your soul.

Regardless of one's attainment or one's astuteness in biblical exposure, a life of prayerlessness causes you to become most vulnerable to the plots and schemes of that old serpent the dragon. As citizens of the kingdom of God, you must at all times immerse yourself in prayer; it is the only means to prepare you for powerful, effective ministry. So, what is it then keeping you from receiving or obtaining power in prayer? Identify then what is it that is obstructing your progress in this matter. There is nothing too great that cannot be conquered if you desire to be an overcomer.

Like everything else, which is important to you, you will make time to include it in your daily routine. Failure to spend time with God is conclusive evidence that at best you will have tragedies unfold and unnecessary.

REMEMBER MY FELLOW KINGDOM AMBASSADORS; PRAYERLESSNESS IS SPIRITUALLY TOXICITY AND A DANGER TO YOUR DESTINATION.

Personal experience: My parental spiritual maturing has led me into a relationship with God through the doorway of prayer. Every morning, before daybreak, my siblings and I were awakened by a resounding call from our parents room, "pra-a-yers," "pra-a-yers." We had to arise, and like soldiers march into their bedroom chamber to pray. There was no option. They firmly believed that a right relationship with Jesus, above all else, includes prayer.

PRAYER:

Loving Father, grant us the help that we seek to identify those areas in our lives that are preventing us from enjoying total intimacy with You, and thereby receiving power to live lives that are pleasing and acceptable unto You. For this is our reasonable service. Here our heartfelt prayer in the name of Him whom You have sent to be "the propitiation for our sins," Jesus Christ the Son of the Living God. Amen!

DEVOTIONAL DAY 1

BROKEN RELATIONSHIP

When something breaks it is not in working condition, it is out of order, it serves no purpose and is of no use. Therefore, it is no longer displayed in its prominent place.

Similarly, a broken relationship with Jesus Christ is lethal to the soul. The longer we stay away from Christ in our brokenness the farther we drift away; and the more difficult it becomes for us to return. It is for this reason inspiration admonishes us that when we sin, we have an advocate with the Father, Jesus Christ the righteousness who is the propitiation for our sins: I John 2:1-2. It is imperative therefore that you make repentance good so that the enemy may not buffer you and cause you to become despondent and fall into his snare.

Whenever your relationship with heavenly Father becomes broken and dysfunctional, you too become weak, vacillating and spiritually impotent. If we are going to restore our relationship and open communications with our Lord, we must daily feed on His nutrients which would allow us to grow and become productive.

It will not suffice us to have outward expressions, but no inward impression of Christ. In other words, a mere profession without a solid possession would lead to a life of duplicity and hypocrisy. Once we develop intimacy with Holy Spirit, fruit bearing is the end result. We must discipline ourselves through much prayer to acquire the virtues of Christ.

Our Savior and Lord is the only source from whom we receive our spiritual vitality and strength. Deficient nutrition results in a lack of spiritual growth and harmonious development. God deeply desires fruitful and lasting intimacy.

Build on your relationship with Holy Spirit today and let Him mend your fragmented heart. You will indeed begin living the abundant life.

Prayer & Meditation

1 Chronicles 16:11

Look to the LORD and his strength;
seek his face always. (NIV)

Prayer Power

Prayer opens the atmosphere of heaven over your life and your nation, causing a spiritual invasion in the earth.

Devotional Day 2

Connect with God

To connect means to bind together, to link, to join or to be joined, or to associate. Through the avenue of prayer you essentially connect with God. We develop friendship through our constant dialogue with Him.

The purpose of prayer is to bring us into oneness with Christ. When we covenant with Him, His purpose for our lives will be accomplished. He is a covenant-keeping God.

Being linked to Holy Spirit enables you to avoid the entanglement of the enemy's machinations and ensures you of a productive future. Note the bible records a very vivid example of a living connection that prophet Elisha had with God in the matter of the king of Syria, II Kings 6:8-22. The record says clearly that Elisha was able to describe even what the king said in his bed chamber. Likewise every believer today as we are in connection with God, we too will be enabled to escape the wiles and snares of the enemy.

You can develop a spiritually holistic and joyous relationship with God. Connect to Him today and reap the benefits.

Prayer & Meditation

St. John 15:7

If ye abide in me, and my words abide in you, ye shall ask what ye will, and it shall be done unto you.

(KJV)

Prayer Power

Prayer is the lynchpin that draws the believer into the very presence of the Divine.

Devotional Day 3

Knowing and Understanding His Word

To know His word is to apprehend, to have clear perception or understanding of, to be sure of or well informed about, or skilled in as a result of study or experience.

To know God's Word is to know God. It is our greatest privilege. Jeremiah 9:23-24a reads, "Thus saith the Lord, Let not the wise man glory in his wisdom, neither let the mighty man glory in his might, let not the rich man glory in his riches: But let him that glorieth glory in that he understandeth and knoweth me."

The only real authority we have is the Word of God, the Bible.

As believers, we must know and understand the word of God, whereby, spiritual growth takes place in our lives. Therefore,

God's word must be made a priority. Our divine purpose should be to know His Word and conform to it.

However, a mere knowing of the word without the accompanying understanding will render you fruitless and confused. It is for this reason that you are admonished, "And with all your getting get understanding," Proverbs 4:7.

Get to know Him through His Word today. For His word is His very breath.

Prayer & Meditation

Psalm 119:11

*Thy word have I hid in mine heart,
that I might not sin against thee. (KJV)*

Prayer Power

Knowing God's Word enables you to pray more effectively based on His Word.

Devotional Day 4

Live in the Spirit

To live is to have life, vitality, vigor, warmth, enjoyment, and brightness. To live in the Spirit is to walk in the Spirit. To walk in the Spirit is to deny the lust of the flesh. You are either led by the spirit or you are led by the flesh.

To live in the Spirit causes one to develop Godly disciplines.

1. Self-control - our emotions, desires, and actions must be subjected to His will. We must have temperance in our daily dealing with others.

2. Word Intake - the most transforming exercise accessible to us is the disciplined ingestion of the Word. This is the most important spiritual discipline. There is no substitute. Knowing the word of God intimately contributes to one living in the Spirit.

3. Meditation - to hear and not meditate is fruitless. Meditation is the best preparation for prayer. When the word of God is taken in, it is digested by meditation and released by prayer. Therefore, meditation of God's word is of great significance in the life of the believer.

When the Holy Spirit lives in us, He works with us "both to will and to do of His good pleasure," Philippians 2:13. "He enlightens the eyes of our understanding," and allows us to know Him in the fullness of the blessedness of Jesus Christ.

Through these disciplines, life in the Spirit will be meaningful.

Prayer & Meditation

Galatians 5:16
This I say then, Walk in the Spirit,
and ye shall not fulfil the lust of the flesh. (KJV)

Self-Control, Word Intake, Meditation—"Spiritual Disciplines for the Christian Life," by author Donald Whitney.

Prayer Power

A life without prayer is equivalent to Spiritual deficit and Imprisonment.

Devotional Day 5

Faith Works Through Love

Faith means to believe or have confidence in. It is a belief that does not require proof or evidence, holds a confident attitude toward God, and involves a commitment to His Will for one's life.

Faith that is motivated by love will always find a way to get to God.

Faith is a developing process. It is built through a prayer foundation. The faith in our lives ought to be built upon each word of God. This causes us to become vulnerable to God. It is faith in God that anchors our love.

Our God requires you to have the kind of faith that moves mountain, yes, but He also requires you to have that kind of faith that is genuinely activated, energized and is propelled by the power of love for God and our fellowmen. Apostle Paul clearly states in I Corinthians 13:2b, "and though I have all faith, so that I could remove mountains, and have not love I am nothing." Faith and love then are two components that are vitally necessary and are highly visible in the life and practice of a matured believer.

A powerful message you can glean from the story of the paralytic demonstrated through his four friends, is that faith demonstrated by love will stop at nothing as you pursue the path that leads into the very presence of God.

Work your faith today with the attitude of love toward God and experience His greatness.

Prayer & Meditation

I Corinthians 13:2

If I have the gift of prophecy and can fathom all mysteries and all knowledge, and if I have a faith that can move mountains, but do not have love, I am nothing. (NIV)

Prayer Power

To Pray in Faith is to receive power to do the will of God that is to love your fellow men.

Devotional Day 6

Perserverance

To persevere means to display a steadfast effort towards following God's commands and doing His work; to persist, or to remain constant for a purpose. It means more than endurance.

Perseverance then, is an essential component require in the development of all Christian virtues. Only in so doing are you strengthened in your character and in your performance.

Therefore, through your persistent pursuit of the profound things of God and your fervency in prayer, your God-given purpose will be accomplished. You must never give up. "I press toward the mark for the prize of the high calling of God which is in Christ Jesus," Phillipians 3:14.

Persevere today and fulfill your dream!

Prayer & Meditation

Hebrews 10:36

You need to persevere so that when you have done the will of God, you will receive what he has promised. (NIV)

Prayer Power

Sincere and fervent prayer invokes heaven's response.

Devotional Day 7

The Revelation of His Word

Revelation is the revealing or disclosing of something which was previously unknown or hidden. It is also an act of God by which He directly imparts truth to the human mind, such knowledge that's beyond man's natural ability to attain.

The written word of God is the complete, all sufficient will of God made known to man through the inspiration of Holy Spirit. The scriptures confirmed that the word of God was not conceived by man, but that holy men of God spake as they were moved by Holy Ghost, II Peter 1:2. This revelatory word then is within itself authoritative, unerring and infallible.

The bible reveals the Son of God who is Himself the Incarnate Word of God, "and the Word became flesh, and dwelt among us; St. John 1:14.

As we submit our whole being to Him, He unfolds His divine will for us and makes our purposes clearer.

Submit your spirit to Him today and walk in His fullness.

Prayer & Meditation

Galatians 1:12

For I neither received it of man, neither was I taught it, but by the revelation of Jesus Christ. (KJV)

Prayer Power

Prayer impregnates your spiritual womb with Visions and Revelation and pushes it through the birth canal.

Devotional Day 8

Believing Fully in the Father

To believe is to have confidence in a statement or promise of another person. To have faith suggests a complete, unquestionable acceptance of something; even in the absence of proof.

"For God so loved the world that He gave His only begotten Son, that whosoever believeth in Him shall not perish but have everlasting life," St. John 3:16.

Jesus in the Holy Scriptures admonishes us to exercise "a child-like faith." That quality of faith which tells us that we must believe fully, completely and unreservedly in what the Father/ Parent says.

No greater demonstration of faith, according to our Savior's own declaration, "I have not found so great faith, no not in Israel." St. Luke 7:9.

To the Father of the faithful Abraham himself, Jehovah promised and fulfilled His promise to him in the birth of his son Isaac. Yet Abraham was called to exhibit even greater faith when he was commanded to offer up Isaac. In this drama God would show that Abraham was fully surrendered in whatever God would have him to do and whatever degree God would have him to go in his walk of faith with God. Hebrews 11:6 says, "But without faith it is impossible to please Him: for he that cometh to God must believe that He is, and that He is a rewarder of them that diligently seek Him."

All He is asking us to do is simply believe. You can experience life in its fullness if you would believe him today.

Prayer & Meditation

Acts 16:31
And they said, "Believe on the Lord Jesus Christ, and thou shalt be saved, and thy house." (KJV)

Prayer Power

Prayer strengthens the soul to believe the unsearchable riches found in the promises of God.

Devotional Day 9

Love Toward the Father

Love is a deep feeling of affection or devotion towards a person. Man's commitment to and desire for God is expressed as Love for Him.

Our greatest commandment is to love God with all we are. As believers, we have the assurance that the Father Himself loves us. With such assurance we can "come boldly" into the very presence of the King of the Universe.

As in nature, this principle is even more so spiritual things, "by beholding we become changed." So the Apostle John calls us to "behold what manner of love the Father hath bestowed upon us," I John 3:1.

Love begat love.

Turn your love toward Him today and let nothing separate you from His love.

Prayer & Meditation

Mark 12:30-31

And thou shalt love the Lord thy God with all thy heart, and with all thy soul, and with all thy mind, and with all thy strength: this is the first commandment. And the second is like, namely this, Thou shalt love thy neighbour as thyself. There is none other commandment greater than these.

(KJV)

Prayer Power

Prayer fills your heart with the love of God and empowers you to demonstrate his unconditional love towards others

Devotional Day 10

The Way to God

Way means a path to, a specific route, or direction. In our world, many are searching for a source of power. The Word of God is the only true source of authority we have. It clearly reveals that the way to God is through Jesus Christ Himself.

How can we know the way? Jesus states in St. John 14:6, "I am the way, the Truth, and the Life, no man cometh unto the Father but by me." The only means by which we can enjoy a tranquil life, and hence possess eternity is through the salvation and redemption brought to us through Jesus Christ.

"For through Him (Jesus), we both have access by one Spirit unto the Father," Ephesians 2:18. We cannot have eternal security with the Father (Jehovah), except we come through the Son (Christ Jesus).

St. John 10 reads, "He that entereth not by the door into the sheepfold, but climbeth up some other way, the same is a thief and a robber. I am the door; by me if any man entereth in, he shall be saved."

Jesus is the only way to God.

Prayer & Meditation

1 Timothy 2:5
For there is one God,
and one mediator between God and men,
the man Christ Jesus; (KJV)

Prayer Power

Failure to pray is a direct disobedience and reveals your unwillingness to allow Holy Spirit's authority in your life.

Devotional Day 11

Abiding in the Vine

Abide means to continue without change; to endure; to last. Jesus is the True Vine. If you abide in Him and His words abide in you, anything you ask will be granted and not denied. However, there is a criterion to be met. You must abide in Christ Jesus.

Our joy is but the outflowing of the strength of the Lord and is nothing more than a manifestation of the mutual symbiotic relationship between the saints and the True Vine.

"I am the Vine, ye are the branches if you remain in me and I in you, you will bear much fruit, apart from me you can do nothing," St. John 15:5 (NIV)

As a result in us giving glory to God in whatever we do our abiding then is not an option or a selection, it is the ordained means of the Father to go and to participate in the fellowship of the Triune God.

Let the fruit abound to your account today as you abide in the Lord.

Prayer & Meditation

John 15:10

If ye keep my commandments, ye shall abide in my love; even as I have kept my Father's commandments, and abide in his love.

Prayer Power

Whereby Prayer causes you to abide in Him, Prayerlessness causes you to be removed from His presence and protection.

Devotional Day 12

The Peace of God

Peace means an undisturbed state of mind, the absence of mental conflict, serenity, and/or tranquility. To experience the peace of God, one's total reliance must be on Him. The Prophet Isaiah declared in chapter 26:3, "Thou wilt keep him in perfect peace, whose mind is stayed on Thee: because he trusted in Thee."

When we, as believers, confidently put our trust in God, He provides for us this supernatural peace that surpasses understanding to the natural mind and sustains us during life's most turbulent moments

How wonderful it is for the believer to know that this grade of peace is available to all who have their minds, their hearts, and their total being centered on Him who is the Prince of Peace. To have the peace of God means to rest fully in Him.

He promised never to leave nor forsake us. "Peace I leave with you, my peace I give unto you not as the world giveth, let not your heart be troubled," St. John 14:27.

We can claim His promise of peace even in the most troublesome of times.

Prayer & Meditation

Phillipians 4:7

And the peace of God, which transcends all understanding, will guard your hearts and your minds in Christ Jesus.

Prayer Power

Prayer grants you Peace in the Midst of Adversity

Devotional Day 13

Commanded to Love

This is my commandment that ye "love one another as I have loved you," St. John 15:12 God does not love us because we are lovable, but because it is His nature to do so. Therefore, He commands us to show that same love one to another.

When we take on the nature of Christ, loving others, especially those who have hurt us, may be difficult but is not impossible.

Having the understanding that God loves us beyond all limits should motivate us to display that same unconditional love towards others.

Despite our differences, despite our feelings, despite our rights, we are commanded to love each other and not let hate consume us. This is how the world will know that we are Disciples of Christ.

The Bible says if we bite and devour one another, take heed that we are not consumed one of another. (Galatians 5:15)

The second greatest commandment is to love your neighbor as yourself. Let the love of Jesus prevail in your heart today.

Prayer & Meditation

Romans 12:10

Be kindly affectioned one to another with brotherly love; in honour preferring one another;

Prayer Power

Consistent praying with a heart of love gives Holy Spirit free range to work on one's' behalf.

Devotional Day 14

Trust His Grace

At some point in our lives as believers, we face issues, concerns that seemingly even after servant prayer still annoy and bewilder us. Often times we find ourselves like the Apostle Paul crying out to God to deliver us from this "thorn in the flesh." What a joyous assurance is ours that like him we can receive from God the assurance that "His grace is sufficient" and that His strength is made perfect in weakness.

Paul faced a similar dilemma and concluded that God had allowed this experience in his life to keep him humble.

Whatever tests the Lord allows He knows that we can bear it. When we perish outwardly we can't lose heart, our spirit man is being renewed and developed for God's glory.

I Corinthians 12:9 says, "His grace is indeed sufficient for us; His strength (power) is made perfect when we are weak."

He wants to break our flesh so His character can be perfected in us. Would you allow him to crush your flesh and bring forth His fragrance?

Trust His grace today.

Prayer & Meditation

Hebrews 4:16

Let us then approach the throne of grace with confidence, so that we may receive mercy and find grace to help us in our time of need.

Prayer Power

Prayerlessness despises the grace of God and mitigates against the work of Holy Spirit in the life of the believer.

Devotional Day 15

Rivers of Living Water
(Becoming a fountain through which the Word can be poured)

River is a natural stream of water that empties itself into an ocean, a lake, or another river. Water is a sitting representation of Holy Spirit.

Jesus says in St. John 7:37-38, "If any man thirst, let him come unto me and drink. He that believeth on me, as the scripture hath said, out of his belly shall flow rivers of living water."

The purpose of water is to give life. We have to become active participants imbibing from that river. We must then develop an unquenchable thirst for the Holy One, submit entirely to His perfect will and practice obedience to all His instructions.

God has called us with a holy calling. Therefore, we must become yielded vessels of honor, sanctified, meet for the Master's use, prepared unto every good work. Only then will the river of God begin to flow through us, and we are able to affect change in the lives of others.

Believe in Him today, you will experience life filled with vigor and you will thereby be empowered to the honor and glory of God.

Let the river flow!

Prayer & Meditation

John 4:14

But whosoever drinketh of the water that I shall give him shall never thirst; but the water that I shall give him shall be in him a well of water springing up into everlasting life.

Prayer Power

Prayer positions you to become a conduit of living waters flowing from your innermost being.

Devotional Day 16

Your Authority in God
(Speaking the Word)

When we do not understand our authority in Christ, we live a life void of power, suffering spiritual defeat under a cloud of satanic inspired depression. Therefore, we must possess our God-given power so that we can live with the dominion God entrusted us with.

Therefore we need to administer the God-given power that we possess, so that we can live with and exercise the dominion that God has entrusted to us.

Our lives will only become productive and prosperous when we understand how to utilize the power God has bestowed upon us. We must fight the enemy with God's Word; decreeing & declaring it over our situations until change takes place.

The bible states in Luke 17:20, "The Kingdom of God is within us, and we have an anointing of the Holy Spirit. Our faith is in the power of the blood of Jesus. Therefore, no weapon formed against us can prosper, Isaiah 54:17.

As we fortify our faith with these words of affirmation, we build our spiritual authority.

The enemy cannot destroy us for this reason; that we know, understand, and exercise our power in God.

Speak His words with authority and live a spirit-filled life.

Prayer & Meditation

Luke 10:19
Look, I have given you authority over all the power of the enemy, and you can walk among snakes and scorpions and crush them. Nothing will injure you.
(NLT)

Prayer Power

Prayer activates the power and authority of God in our lives, and gives us dominion in the earth realm.

Devotional Day 17

Alive unto God

The Apostle Paul wrote in the book of Romans chapter 6:10-11, "For in that He died, He died unto sin once, in that He liveth, He liveth unto God; Likewise reckon ye also yourselves to be dead indeed unto sin, but alive unto God through Jesus Christ our Lord."

If we want the life of Christ, we must be ready to give up our lives. In dying to sin, we must unrobe ourselves of all fleshly lusts and desires; and wholly submit our will to God. Jesus said, "If any man comes after me, he must deny himself, take up his cross and follow me," Matthew 16:24. In other words, surrender all to the perfect will of God. (Not my will, but Thine be done).

Paul said in Galatians 2:20, "I am crucified with Christ: nevertheless I live; yet not I, but Christ liveth in me:" Before we can fully experience the life of Christ within, our old man with his deeds must be put to death. There must be a demise before there can be a rebirth.

As saints of God, we must make up our minds to go all the way with Christ. All the way means, giving up everything we hold dear to us and entirely yield to Christ alone. If we are genuinely willing to walk in His way, then there is a price we must pay. EVERYTHING. All that we are, all that we own, and all that we love... then and only then, will we have the life of Christ within.

Give Him your all today and live life in abundance.

Prayer & Meditation

1 Peter 2:24

Who his own self bare our sins in his own body on the tree, that we, being dead to sins, should live unto righteousness: by whose stripes ye were healed.

Prayer Power

Prayer ignites the life of the Spirit within the believer to pursue God in His fullness.

Devotional Day 18

He Restores My Soul

To restore means to bring back to its original state. Restoration comes with true repentance. Hosea 6:1-2 declares, "Come, let us return (repent) to the Lord! He has torn us in pieces; now He will heal us. He has injured us; now He will bandage our wounds. In just a short time, He will restore (make us whole) so we can live in His presence."

We have strayed far from God's presence because of the sin that has stealthily and imperceptibly invaded our lives. The soul becomes restless and seeks to regain intimate love and relationship that it once experienced. The cry is heard with great pathos "Have mercy upon me O God, according to Thy loving kindness: according to the multitude of Thy tender mercies blot out my transgressions."

We've allowed hurts to turn into bitterness and hatred, and unforgiveness has entrenched us.

I submit to you, that if you would take one moment and reflect on David's appeal in Psalm 51, God will restore you today. He is waiting for you to recognize your need for His grace and mercy. Come before Him with a heart of sincere repentance. "A broken and contrite heart He will not despise," Psalm:51:17.

He is longing to restore unto you the joy of His salvation, and lead you in the path of righteousness.

Return to Him today, He will refresh you with His presence and make you completely whole.

Prayer & Meditation

Psalms 51:12

Restore unto me the joy of your salvation; and uphold me with your free spirit.

Prayer Power

Prayer is the entering wedge in the path of Restoration.

Devotional Day 19

Watchman on the Wall
(Intercessor)

Watchman – one who guards or keeps watch. Watchmen are people given to intercession. They are persistent pray-ers who are loyal and committed to standing in the gap for others. Intercessors are granted influence over nations.

It is expected that we pray continuously for our families and loved ones and the body of Christ at large. While this is good because of our influence, we also have the obligation to pray for the leaders of our nations as demanded in scriptures. 1Timothy 2:1-2 says, I exhort therefore, that, first of all, supplications, prayers, intercessions and giving of thanks be made for all men, for kings and for all that are in authority;"

We need not be concerned with all of the political intrigue and blatant political corruptions of the nations. Society is impacted and influenced to become a better place to live in.

The Bible says in II Chronicles 7:14, "If my people which are called by my name, will humble themselves and pray, seek my face, turn from their wicked ways, then I will hear from heaven, and will forgive their sins and heal their land."

In order for God to move on our behalf, we ought to maintain the proper attitudes of humility, repentance, and obedience. When these conditions are met, God brings healing to our land.

Stay on the wall, and you will gain favorable results.

Prayer & Meditation

Ezekial 2:20

And I sought for a man among them,
that should make up the hedge,
and stand in the gap before me for the land,
that I should not destroy it: but I found none.

Prayer Power

Prayer is the bedrock of the believer and can shift the course of nations.

Devotional Day 20

Being Reconciled to God

Reconcile - to bring into harmony, to make friendly again, to settle something. It possesses the idea to change thoroughly. To be completely altered or adjusted to a required standard.

Reconciliation is the process by which God and His people are brought back together again. The Bible teaches us that we have been alienated from one another because of God's holiness and human sinfulness. God took the initiative in reconciling us back to Him when He sent Christ to die for us in our sinful state. Paul said in Romans that, "When we were yet sinners and enemies, Christ died." II Corinthians 5:19 says, "to wit, that God was in Christ reconciling the world to Himself, not imputing their trespasses unto them; and hath committed unto us the word of reconciliation."

Friends, the way has already been made. Our sins have

separated us from having a meaningful relationship with God. Today is a new opportunity to settle an old account.

Ask the Lord to wash you, make you clean, and bring you into a renewed fellowship with Him. Now is the accepted time, now is the day of salvation, if you will hear His voice, harden not your heart.

Be ye reconciled today.

Prayer & Meditation

2 Corinthians 5:18

And all things are of God, who hath reconciled us to himself by Jesus Christ, and hath given to us the ministry of reconciliation;

Prayer Power

Prayerlessness remove one's desire to be reconciled to God and others

Devotional Day 21

Courage in Suffering

The patriarch David throughout his lifetime has been, for the people of God, a supreme example of courage even courage in suffering. Our attention is drawn to the riveting experience of David at Ziklag where under the threat of mutiny and assassination by his own account "he encouraged himself in the Lord." Behold the anointed king crying out to God in the midst of intense suffering. How like him should every child of God under severe stress and threats of annihilation take courage and be strong in the Lord and in the power of His might.

Courage then to the believer is as natural as the brilliancy of the sun.

Take heart dear believer, God knows all about your sufferings and your struggles and He is well able to deliver. You are more than a conqueror through Christ who loves you.

Know that He will not only rescue you, but will hide you in a secure place where the enemy cannot touch you. A place where you will experience real and lasting freedom.

Take courage, my friend, don't you dare lose heart. Press your way through!

Prayer & Meditation

Romans 8:18

I consider that our present sufferings are not worth comparing with the glory that will be revealed in us.

Prayer Power

Prayer gives you strength to endure suffering, and courage to go forward.

Devotional Day 22

Hearing and Obeying
(The Word of God)

St. Matthew 7:24 & 26 reads, "therefore whosoever heareth these sayings of mine, and doeth them, I will liken Him unto a wise man, which buildeth his house upon a rock: And everyone that heareth these sayings of mine, and doeth them not, shall be likened unto a foolish man, which built his house upon the sand."

There are two divisions of the hearers of God's word. Those that hear and take action and those that hear but do nothing. To hear Christ is to obey Him. Hearing His words is useless unless we put them into practice. When we do not follow what we hear, we receive the grace of God in vain.

To obey Christ is to give heed to His word and in so doing; we conscientiously abstain from anything that would bring reproach and dishonor to His Holy name. "Behold to obey is better than sacrifice, and to hearken than the fat of rams." I Samuel 15:22.

The Lord has not left us ignorant as to what He would have us to do in addition to hearing His word, "but to do justly, to love mercy and to walk humbly with Thy God." Micah 6:8.

Doubtless it is not sufficient to be hearers of the Word only but we must possess those sterling active godly energies that propel us to do what does saith the Lord.

Walk in obedience to the word that you hear!

Prayer & Meditation

James 1:22

But be ye doers of the word, and not hearers only, deceiving your own selves.

Prayer Power

A life of prayer gives one the impetus to hear God's word and obey it.

Devotional Day 23

Suffering to Become Like Him

Suffering means agony, affliction, or distress, intense pain or sorrow. Believers share in the suffering of Christ, so as through pain they will identify with Him.

Suffering is indeed an essential inescapable part of the Christian experience. Our Savior assures us that in this world we shall have tribulation. The Apostle Paul in the book of II Timothy 3:12 says that, "Yea, and all that will live godly in Christ Jesus shall suffer persecution."

Christ wore the armor of love, joy, peace, patience, forgiveness, kindness, meekness, gentleness and self-control.

As believers, it is our desire and determination to become Christ-like and walk according to His divine purpose for our lives. Because of this we must be spiritually prepared to embrace suffering.

Peter went on to say, "For he that hath suffered in the flesh hath ceased from sin; that he no longer should live the rest of his time in the flesh to the lusts of men, but to the will of God." (1 Peter 4:1-2)

In the midst of the enemy's viral and debilitating attacks, thank God that we are not left to combat with Him on our own and in our own strength.

My dear friends, go through your suffering with patience, it will be well worth it.

Prayer & Meditation

1 Peter 5:10

But the God of all grace, who hath called us unto his eternal glory by Christ Jesus, after that ye have suffered a while, make you perfect, stablish, strengthen, settle you.

Prayer Power

Prayer is like a pain killer that soothes us in time of trials and persecutions.

Devotional Day 24

Shake It Off

Throughout our walk with God, many times the enemy through false accusations, rumors, and scandals, viciously attacks us. He aims to keep us from entering into a close relationship with God.

I'm reminded of the story of Paul in Acts 28 after he was shipwrecked. While putting a bundle of sticks into a fire to warm himself, a poisonous viper came out of the fire and fastened itself onto Paul's hand.

Those who stood around expected Paul to swell up and die. This is the enemy's plan for us as believers. His studied purpose is to produce affliction that causes hatred and a desire for revenge, malice, and all kinds of ungodly traits.

If we allow ourselves to become infected and puffed (swollen) up with these symptoms, it causes spiritual death. Paul simply shook it off.

The deep hurt you have experienced that continues to torment your mind, causing resentment, and offensiveness, my friends, shake it off.

Release hostility and animosity to the Lord today. Do not allow these poisons to penetrate your spirit, which is exactly what the enemy wants to happen. Replace them with the fruit of the spirit, recorded in Gal. 5:21, love, joy, peace, longsuffering, gentleness, goodness, faith, meekness and self-control.

You are more than a conqueror. You will not be defeated nor denied if you shake it off.

Prayer & Meditation

1 Peter 3:10
For, "Whoever would love life and see good days must keep their tongue from evil and their lips from deceitful speech.

Prayer Power

Prayer places an invisible shield of protection around your heart

Devotional Day 25

Deliverance

Over two thousand years ago, Jesus delivered us from the power and authority of Satan into the loving power of Almighty God. He paid the ultimate price for our redemption. He freed us from the dominion of sin and Satan's wrath by the exchange of His life.

The shedding of His blood on Calvary was the ransom paid. He gave His life that we might have an abundantly blessed life. The problem is some of us are still living in darkness and don't realize that we have been delivered.

Colossians 1:13-14 states, "who hath delivered us from the power of darkness, and translated us into the kingdom of His dear Son: In whom we have redemption through His blood, even the forgiveness of sins."

It is evident that we as the body of Christ are not walking in the victory that Christ has already won for us.

I encourage you today to grasp this revelation of truth, that you have been delivered, and start living in the light.

Prayer & Meditation

Colossians 1:13
Who hath delivered us from the power of darkness, and hath translated us into the kingdom of his dear Son: (KJV)

Prayer Power

PRAYERLESSNESS ENGAGES SIN AND HINDERS THE DELIVERANCE PROCESS OF SELF, FAMILIES, REGIONS, NATIONS AND TERRITORIES.

Devotional Day 26

Praise that Moves God

Praise is a kin to worship. It is more than just a mere expression of worship, but it is in essence the engine if you please, of the worship experience. All true worship is undergirded with praise.

When we become true praisers, our thoughts and aspirations are toward God and not ourselves. Indeed the hallelujah is for Jesus. Psalm 22:3 says, "But Thou art holy, O Thou that inhabitest the praises of Israel." This particular Psalm informs us that God is more than just ecstatic with and by the praises of His creatures, and that wherever our God is praise is naturally to follow.

Our praises, our individual acclamation and our approbation that exalts, justly so and extolls the virtue of a Holy God. In other words, God designs that each praiser would offer up praises to Him that are unique in and of itself. Our God is in no way ill-pleased or is blushful when we through the praise of His name serenade Him in song and in praise.

And so let everything that hath breath praise the Lord!

Prayer & Meditation

Psalms 138:1-2

I will praise Thee with my whole heart: before the gods will I sing praises unto Thee. I will worship toward Thy holy temple, and praise Thy name for Thy lovingkindness and for Thy truth:

Prayer Power

The Power of Prayer through Praise moves the hand of Omnipotence.

Devotional Day 27

What is obstructing your flow?

To obstruct means to block up, build against, clog, hinder (progress or activity). Believers today are confronted with a multiplicity of challenging issues deigned to create interference, interruption and indiscretion. Hence he/she are left to the buffeting of his/her soul.

In order to move forward, one must need deal squarely and effectively with those areas of pain (deep pain) and to find relief and release in the promise of our God.

It is no mystery therefore how our God uses this unfortunate state of many of His erring children, He calls us to "behold," look, the Lord's hand is not shortened, that it cannot save, neither His ear heavy, that it cannot hear. But your iniquities have separated between you and your God, and your sins have hid His face from you, that He will not hear. Isaiah 59:1-2.

Sin then is the only clogging material that comes between the soul and the Savior and can only be removed if we desire it to be.

Repent and allow Holy Spirit to remove the clutter because He will not flow through a clogged pipe.

Prayer & Meditation

Jeremiah 30:17

For I will restore health unto thee, and I will heal thee of thy wounds, saith the LORD; because they called thee an Outcast, saying,
This is Zion, whom no man seeketh after.

Prayer Power

Genuine Prayer and Repentance effectively eliminate the blockages from your life.

Devotional Day 28

CONSECRATE YOURSELVES

To consecrate means to set apart as holy, or to make and declare sacred for religious use, or to devote entirely.

Leviticus 20:7-8 states, "Consecrate yourselves and be holy, because I am the Lord your God. Keep my decrees and follow them. I am the Lord who makes you holy."

Sanctification is indeed the work of a lifetime. It cannot be obtained in a moment of time. Holiness is synonymous with sanctification. We are reminded that without holiness no man would see the Lord. Individually our vessels ought to be free from defilement in its varied genre, "it is what comes out of a man that makes him unclean." For from within, out of men's heart come evil thoughts, sexual immorality, theft, murder, adultery greed, malice, deceit, lewdness, envy, slander, arrogance and folly.

Sanctification is as much a command in scripture as the command by our Savior to love one another. We are required to be sanctified. Isaiah 8:13 says, "Sanctify the Lord of Hosts Himself; and let Him be your fear, and let Him be your dread."

Allow the Lord to consecrate you today so that you can be fit for His kingdom.

Prayer & Meditation

Psalms 51:7
Purge me with hyssop, and I shall be clean: wash me, and I shall be whiter than snow.

Prayer Power

A life without Prayer is a mockery of Sanctification.

Devotional Day 29

Never Doubt God

Doubt is a feeling of uncertainty or a lack of conviction. Doubt is the opposite of faith and the scripture makes it abundantly clear that what is not of faith in sin. Romans 14:23.

If there is one sin God hates more than the other, it is the sin of doubt and unbelief. It grieves the Lord. It is nothing less than faithlessness; and without faith it is impossible to please God. Doubt is very offensive to God and it causes you to live a life of uncertainty.

The entire episode of the entrance of sin finds its basis in the man (Adam) doubting the word of God over against that of the enemy. In other words, sin began with doubting the clear unalterable, unerring word of Jehovah.

The final analysis is that when you doubt, you are questioning the integrity and character of God.

The word of God like the nature of God, it is changeless, it is permanent, it is everlasting, it is eternal. Therefore we base our trust and have confidence in His unchanging, un-altering word.

This is the sacrifice pleasing unto Him.

Prayer & Meditation

Numbers 23:19

Numbers 23:19 says, "God is not a man, that He should lie, neither the son of man that He should repent: hath He said, and shall He not do it? Or hath He spoken, and shall He not make it good?

Prayer Power

Prayer is the fuel that propels the engine of trust and dispels doubt.

Devotional Day 30

The Wise in Character

he bible says in Proverbs 9:9, "Instruct a wise man and he will be wiser still, teach a righteous man, he will add to his learning."

It is intriguing to note that wherever the scripture makes reference to wisdom or being wise, almost immediately thereafter or not too far from, wisdom is connected to humility or having a teachable spirit. The book of Proverbs is pregnant with such examples. The Prophet Micah picks up the same theme in chapter 6:8-9. God calls His people to be wise and not otherwise.

True wisdom is enlightening, illuminating and powerful. When wisdom is applied to the Christian life, the individual becomes teachable, willing to be humbled for the honor and glory of God. It is the true test of Christian character.

The character of the wise person embraces that discipline and learning are life-long goals.

A wise person should always be in an atmosphere of humility.

Prayer & Meditation

James 1:5

If any of you lack wisdom, let him ask of God, that giveth to all men liberally, and upbraideth not; and it shall be given him.

Prayer Power

WISDOM IS TO PRAYER WHAT BREATH IS TO THE SOUL.

www.ingramcontent.com/pod-product-compliance
Lightning Source LLC
Chambersburg PA
CBHW070622300426
44113CB00010B/1619